BIBL

A COTSWOL

Arlington Mill from the River Coln

Published by
REARDON PUBLISHING
(Reardon & Son Publishers)
56 Upper Norwood Street, Leckhampton
Cheltenham, Glos, GL53 ODU

Copyright © 1995
REARDON & SON

Fully Revised 2nd Edition 1997
Revised 3rd Edition 1999

Cover Photographs
Julia Craig

Author
Joanna E.Dee

ISBN 1 873877 13 7
www.reardon.co.uk

Maps & illustrations
Peter T.Reardon

Layout & Design
Nicholas Reardon

Printed by
STOATE & BISHOP (Printers) Ltd
Cheltenham, Glos.

THE ESSENCE OF BIBURY

If you come to Bibury early in the morning, as the mist rolls gently back from the hills surrounding the village, and you walk along the banks of the gently flowing River Coln, you will find a row of traditional Cotswold cottages, well known throughout England, and indeed the world. This row of weavers' cottages is known as Arlington Row, and is perhaps one of the most photographed places in the Cotswolds.

Welcome to Bibury.

William Morris once described Bibury as "the most beautiful village in England." It is a very special village, with a character of its own, but with a tradition and feel that is purely Cotswold. Many people return to Bibury, time and time again, breathing in the beauty and the tranquillity of the river meandering through the Coln Valley, with the enchanting, Cotswold stone cottages and old Mills.

Bibury is really two places. Arlington lies to the west of the river, and Bibury itself over the bridge to the east. Bibury has been considered a suitable spot for human habitation since prehistoric times, as the old burial mounds found on the road up to Ablington testify. The Romans settled near Bibury, in the ancient town of Cirencester (Corinium). In A.D. 725-740, the Bishop of Worcester granted 15 casates of land on the River Coln to Earl Leppa and his daughter Beage. Her name was used in the place name 'Beaganbyrig', and this was recorded in the Domesday book. Gradually this name changed over the centuries until it became Bibury.

During the Middle Ages, Bibury was badly hit by the plague, and as a result a great change in inhabitants was recorded. Many people came to the area to look for work, as there was great poverty. It seems likely that there may also have been an epidemic of a sheep disease, as the soil was unnaturally infertile, indicating a lack of sheep to manure the ground.

At the time of the dissolution of the monasteries during Henry VIII's reign, a great change took place in Bibury, as was happening elsewhere in England. Up until that time Bibury had belonged to the Church, but when

Edward VI came to power in 1547, the village was sold to a Mr. John Harrington for the sum of £225, thus passing to lay ownership, having been an ecclesiastical property for over 800 years. For what now seems a small sum of money John Harrington became the proud owner of the whole of the Manor of Bibury, the Church and the Rectory.

A Monastery was founded at Bibury in the 18th Century. The founding of such monasteries and churches throughout the Cotswold at this time not only indicates increasing Christianisation and purification of the area, but since many monasteries were the centres of large agricultural estates, it also reflects a society which was able, organised and willing enough to draw upon its agricultural surplus for their building works.

Bibury prospered during the period of the 17th and 18th centuries due to the wool trade. At that time Cotswold sheep were considered to produce the finest wool in Europe, the 'Golden Fleece'. However a little later in the 18th century the wool trade went into decline, heralding the end of this period of wealth. A second source of income for the village was from quarrying the local stone, which was much in demand for building work. Most of the Bibury stone cottages you see to-day date from this prosperous period, when they were built to replace less substantial wooden houses. In 1770 money was raised by subscription to build a stone bridge over the River Coln, prior to this date everyone had to ford the icy river.

From 1830 the Cotswolds saw a deepening depression as a decline in wages, the enclosure of common land and advances in mechanised farming deepened the poverty of the Cotswold agricultural labourer. Gloucestershire became the centre for a number of riots and attacks of arson, known as the 'Swing Riots' (so named after a Captain Swing whose name appeared on threatening letters sent to landlords who bought new machinery to replace their labour force). An automated threshing machine was set alight in Tetbury, and this was closely followed by other similar incidents in Bibury and other Cotswold villages. Some Bibury residents were arrested and transported to penal colonies in Australia.

To-day Bibury is a serene village which has weathered the ups and downs of history well. It is a popular place for tourists to visit, being both tranquil and pretty, but also able to offer places of interest to visit and enjoyable walks in and around the village. Every stone seems to have a history, and perhaps it is this feeling that makes Bibury so unique.

What do we find in Bibury as we walk through the village?

Bibury Court originates from Tudor times. The building, as we see it to-day was built by Thomas and Barbara Sackville in 1633 (their initials can still be seen over the front porch). The manor passed down through the Sackville family (an illegitimate descendant of the Earl of Dorset) by female line to the Creswells. Escourt Creswell was M.P. for Cirencester from 1768 to 1774. Part of the estate was sold to Lord Sherborne in 1816, and in 1925 it was sold to Sir Orme Clarke. Bibury Court became a country hotel in 1968, and is now owned and managed by the Johnson family.

Bibury Court

When you come into Bibury from Coln St. Aldwyn there is a breathtaking view of the Bibury Court Hotel and the old village of Bibury from the top of the hill. It is well worth a walk up this country road to enjoy the panorama.

Arlington Row is an almost perfect example of typical Cotswold cottages. Set running up a small hill from the banks of the River Coln, they make a marvellously picturesque scene. Arlington Row was once a timber-framed wool hall, built to hold the wool from the Bishop of Worcester's flocks. There was a 'caretaker' in residence to guard the wool, as evidenced by a smoke blackened wall indicating that a fire was used to keep someone warm. The wool hall was converted into weaver's cottages during the prosperous seventeenth century, and the weavers who lived and worked there washed and dyed their cloth in the stone troughs by the mill leat that runs in front of the Row. To-day nearly all the cottages are owned and preserved by the National Trust. To the right of Arlington Row you can see a tiny little Cotswold cottage called 'The Dolls House'.

ARLINGTON ROW — BIBURY.   REARDON

Rack Isle is so named because it is an area where cloth was 'racked' to dry after fulling (washing) and dyeing. The cloth was stretched on 'tenters', and this is where the word tenterhooks derives from! Rack Isle is now a wildfowl reserve and home to many varied species of birds and flora and fauna. Rack Isle lies to the West of the Coln River, and in the summer presents an array of wild flowers, insects and birds.

The Swan Hotel was first recorded in the seventeenth century, but the present building dates from the nineteenth century, with the large wing to the left of the building added in the 1930s. The Manor Court used to be held in the Swan, and a testimony to this is the windowless octagonal building with a heavy door beside the parking spaces at the end of the hotel, which used to be the village prison! The prisoners were held overnight here before being transported to larger jails in the area. Other forms of punishment for small crimes were either a day in the stocks, or a ducking on a 'ducking stool' into the river. More serious crimes were dealt with at the County Assize Court.

The Swan has been a favourite watering hole for Biburians for many decades, and even attracted visitors from further afield such as Cirencester and Stroud. It recently underwent a complete refurbishment programme to a high standard, and offers visitors every comfort.

The Swan Hotel

The Trout Farm sits just across the bridge from the Swan Hotel. If you want to see wildlife of all varieties at close quarters; from herons to kingfishers, water voles to the occasional mink, glimpses of native brown trout, grayling and of course the famed Rainbow Trout, the Farm is a wonderful, place to visit! It was founded on the site of the old water cress beds in 1902 by Arthur Severn, a well-known naturalist and grandson of a Joseph Severn. Records state that through Joseph, Arthur was related to John Ruskin the Poet who was with Keats in Rome when he was on his Death-Bed.

Kingfisher in Flight

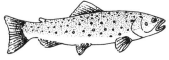

The Trout. A popular fresh-water fish

A Water Vole by the river

As one of the oldest, and certainly the best known trout farm in the Country, Bibury's beautifully landscaped setting belies the enormous amount of work which goes on behind the scenes. Each year up to ten million Rainbow Trout eggs may be spawned with outlets for about one third throughout the U.K. and occasionally abroad. The remainder are grown on until they reach the requisite size usually within one to two years. Renowned for their superb quality and 'fighting' ability the principal market for Bibury's trout is to supply or 'restock' lakes and reservoirs the length and breadth of England and Wales. Visitors to the trout farm are able to feed them and see the water boil in a frenzy of 'troghte' (Greek for greed). There is a small fishery where trout may be caught or alternately they may be purchased at the 'Rainbows End' fish counter alongside other mouth watering produce such as smoked trout, pates, wines, preserves etc. An attractive gift shop, plant sales area, refreshments, explanatory notices and picnic spots sprinkled around the farm ensure that there is something to satisfy the needs of everyone. The farm is open all year around, and a free car park is now available on the Ablington Road (turn left by the Swan Hotel).

Arlington Mill stands overlooking the Trout Farm, its huge bulk re-enforced by massive buttresses constructed in the mid-nineteenth century. The present Mill dates from the seventeenth century, although the Domesday survey of 1086 records two mills in Arlington, but this may just indicate that there were two millstones under one roof. Arlington Mill was one of the biggest corn mills in the area during the nineteenth century, and a steam engine was brought in to assist the massive water wheel, running six grinding stones. For a short time in the 1600s the mill was used for 'fulling' (cleaning) the wool cloth produced by the weavers at Arlington Row.

Arlington Mill has not been used as a corn mill since 1913. The machinery was dismantled in 1914 and the metal was used for armaments in the First World War. At the same time the Miller's rights passed to the Trout Farm next door, which meant the water flow to the mill was reduced, in order to supply the fish farm. This also meant that there was insufficient water to drive any machinery again. For many years the building was used solely for storage until David Verey, an architectural historian bought the building and set about restoring it and turning it into a Museum. He found replacement Mill machinery on the Bathurst Estate (which runs on an electric motor) and also found a small waterwheel at a nearby pub - neither the machinery nor the wheel are in any way comparable to the original huge corn milling machinery that originally worked the mill, but his farsightedness did much to restore the heart of this fine Mill.

Tragically David Verey died in 1984, but his family kept the Museum open for the next ten years before selling it. Early in 1995, after a change of ownership, the mill machinery was totally overhauled, and new displays and exhibitions were set up showing something of the history of the mill and Bibury, how the machinery works (with hands-on examples for people to try). A general updating and renovation programme has been carried out. The mill now boasts an attractive tearoom with outside terrace by the millstream and a well-stocked and interesting gift shop. A new addition is an enchanting herb garden behind the mill, this Garden is included in the Museum entrance ticket, and is a delightful place to sit and enjoy a warm summer's day.

The Catherine Wheel is a delightful 15th Century Inn which can be found up the hill from Arlington Mill. It contains massive ships timbers as beams, and has lovely old stone walls and log fires burning on chilly days. It has an outstanding reputation for good food and friendliness and is a firm favourite with both locals and tourists.

THE
CATHERINE WHEEL

The

DIANE BREEN GALLERY

Bibury's art gallery, in a picturesque setting overlooking the river Coln, is just a brief stroll downstream from Arlington Row.

Here you will find original paintings and limited edition prints by Bibury's resident artist Diane Breen, and a wide selection of work by acclaimed Cotswold and national artists such as Lesley Holmes, Anuk Naumann, Anne Cotterill and Paul Riley.

plus

Unusual ceramics, hand made glassware, textiles and other fine giftware

Summer Opening 10.30am - 5pm Wednesday to Monday
Closed Tuesday
Winter Opening 11am - 4.30pm Wednesday to Sunday
Closed Monday & Tuesday
(other times by appointment)

15 The Street, Bibury, Glos. GL7 5NP - Telephone 01285 740736

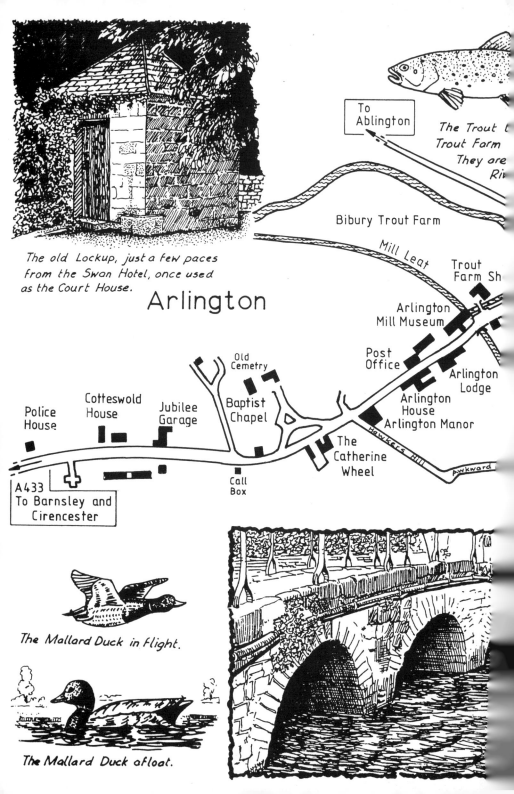

The old Lockup, just a few paces from the Swan Hotel, once used as the Court House.

Arlington

To Ablington

The Trout
Trout Farm
They are
Riv

Bibury Trout Farm

Mill Leat

Trout Farm Sh

Arlington Mill Museum

Post Office

Arlington Lodge

Arlington House

Arlington Manor

Hawkers Hill

Awkward

Old Cemetery

Baptist Chapel

The Catherine Wheel

Police House

Cotteswold House

Jubilee Garage

Call Box

A433 To Barnsley and Cirencester

The Mallard Duck in flight.

The Mallard Duck afloat.

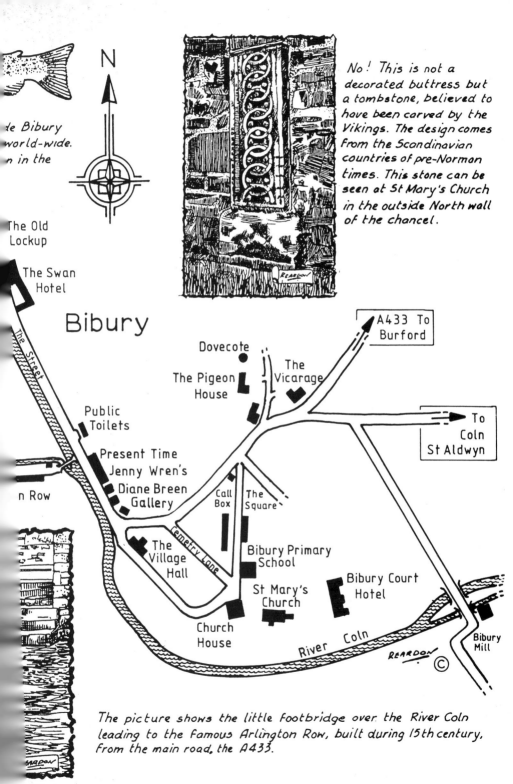

No! This is not a decorated buttress but a tombstone, believed to have been carved by the Vikings. The design comes from the Scandinavian countries of pre-Norman times. This stone can be seen at St Mary's Church in the outside North wall of the chancel.

N

...de Bibury
...world-wide.
...n in the

The Old Lockup

The Swan Hotel

The Street

Bibury

A433 To Burford

Dovecote

The Pigeon House

The Vicarage

To Coln St Aldwyn

Public Toilets

Present Time
Jenny Wren's
Diane Breen Gallery

...n Row

Call Box

The Square

Cemetry Lane

The Village Hall

Bibury Primary School

St Mary's Church

Bibury Court Hotel

Church House

River Coln

REARDON ©

Bibury Mill

The picture shows the little footbridge over the River Coln leading to the famous Arlington Row, built during 15th century, from the main road, the A433.

ARLINGTON MILL MUSEUM
AT BIBURY

The Domesday Book shows there was a Mill on the banks of the
Coln as long ago as 1068.
The current Mill dates back to the 17th century, and its fascinating
history can be traced through pictures, photographs and documents.
There are examples of milling and the Victorian way of life, and you
can see the working machinery which is over 200 years old
Examine the efficiency of cogs, wheels, pulleys and water power.
Meet the *"Ghost of the Grey Lady"*, follow the *"Tale of the Arlington
Cat"*, and see a *"Swing Riot Hanging"*.

HERB GARDEN
TEA ROOM, GIFT SHOP
&
LICENSED RESTAURANT
with lovely Millstream Terrace

Arlington Mill, Bibury, Nr Cirencester, Glos, GL7 NL
Tel: (01285) 740368

St. Mary's Church is found on the Bibury side of the River Coln. If you walk down Cemetery Lane you will find it tucked behind the Bibury Court Hotel. The Church has been added to many times over the centuries, but in origin it is late Saxon. The shell of the Saxon building is marked by pilaster strips on the North and South walls of the chancel, probably indicating the original eastern extent. There is part of a Saxon cross on the exterior of the Church on the North wall, and inside the church has some casts of Saxon grave slabs.

In the eighth century, St. Mary's belonged to the Bishop of Worcester, and then passed to the Abbey of Oseney in Oxford in 1130. The windows on the side were added in the fourteenth century to give the interior of the church more light. There is evidence of the importance of this Church in the area, the priest held an unusually large holding of land (some 360 acres), and fragments of expensive glass have been found near to the Church indicating the substance and high cost of building. A further indication of the continuing importance of St. Mary's Church is the size of the rich wool merchants tombs to be found in the graveyard.

There is a legend that there was a painting of St. Christopher on the wall of the Church, the sight of which, according to the monks, would preserve you from violent or sudden death.

There is an interesting story connected with an area of St. Mary's church-yard called the 'Bisley Piece'. Twice the parish of Bisley fell into disfavour with the Bishop of Worcester. Once for allowing their priest to fall down an uncovered well in the churchyard, and again for a fight in the churchyard which resulted in blood being spilt on consecrated ground. For a period, the Bisley dead were not allowed to be buried in the Diocese of Worcester. Bibury was the only parish within a huge area not under this jurisdiction, so the bodies of the Bisley dead had to be carried fifteen miles to Bibury, and buried in the 'Bisley Piece'.

Bibury Race Course used to hold regular race meetings. It was located four miles up the road at Ladbarrow, between Hatherop and Coln St. Aldwyns. Some say that the races started in 1681, and the exclusive Bibury club was the first of its kind in England and had its origin in Whitsuntide gaieties. King

Charles II transferred the Newmarket spring meeting to Bibury and attended it with his mistress, Nell Gwynne. It was also attended by George IV when he was the Prince of Wales. However, as Newmarket grew in popularity, so Bibury racecourse's popularity declined, and to-day there is scarcely a trace of its existence. Although a Bibury race meeting still existed at the beginning of the twentieth century, it was not held in Bibury, but was held at Salisbury racecourse - the view was over the Salisbury plain, not over the Cotswolds.

Dragonfly   Moorhen

The Mute Swan —and— in flight

Roman Villa. There is evidence of a large Roman villa in the valley south east of Bibury Court, probably built in the Third Century. Fragments of mosaic pavement, glass and masonry have been found. No doubt the Romans were attracted by the sheltered valley and the fish for food in the River Coln, and it was close to their nearby settlement in Cirencester. This villa has never been excavated, but it seems to be large and luxurious and was said to have central heating. The villa was discovered at the end of the nineteenth century quite by accident, when preparations were being made for the burial of a deceased cow!

The Swan Hotel

There probably hasn't been a time when a hostelry of some sort hasn't been on the site of The Swan Hotel. We can date parts of the building back to 1640.

Nowadays, The Swan has become synonymous with elegance and luxury, with friendly service making us ideal for short breaks, family parties or a base for touring the Cotswolds.

The 18 individually designed bedrooms, three with Four-poster beds have lavish bathrooms, some with double Jacuzzi's. Fresh flowers, Home-made Cottage Biscuits and bottles of local Spring Water complete these lovely rooms.

Our AA Rosetted Signet Room is arguable one of the finest in the Cotswolds. Sundays see a traditional menu for lunch with dinners presenting a regularly changing menu of Modern English style. We use only the finest produce, local where possible.

We welcome non-residents in the The Swan Bar, pop in just to see the "famous mural" or try one of the local Real Ales. During the summer Bar meals are served in the Courtyard.

Two Conference rooms, Licensed for Civil Marriages, Private Fishing on the River Coln and private Riverside Garden for our residents make the Swan the place to be.

Let us share The Swan Experience with YOU !!
Tel 01285 740695, Fax 01285 740473, e-mail - swanhotl@swanhotel-cotswolds.co.uk
website: http://www.swanhotel.co.uk

Byberry, U.S.A. In the year 1675, four brothers - Nathaniel, Thomas, Daniel and William Walton left Bibury and travelled across the Atlantic by ship, landing at Newcastle in the U.S.A. They were part of a group of settlers from Bibury suffering from persecution, who went to America. They crossed the ocean to found new homes, and be at liberty to worship God in their own way. During the latter part of the seventeenth century there was persecution and trial for all who were not members of the established church. An early entry in the Baptist Church book at Arlington records 'There was nonconformist preaching at Bibury'.

The brothers had worked together in Arlington Mill, and stayed together when they got to America, proceeding up the Delaware Valley. They were impressed with the fertile land, and selected a spot for their new home. This same spot was included seven years later in William Penn's plans for Philadelphia. It is recounted that the Waltons determined the name of their town by each of them placing a name in a hat. The first name out of the hat was 'Byberry'.

PRESENT TIME at Bibury
Gloucestershire

BIBURY COURT HOTEL

Morning Coffee - Light Lunches - Afternoon Teas - Dinners

Set in its own grounds by the river Coln on the outskirts of Bibury directly behind the Church

Telephone (01285) 740337 / 324 Fax (01285) 740660

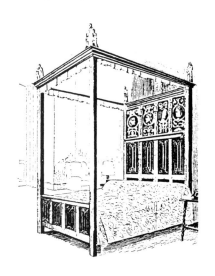

Bibury Court is a beautiful Mansion dating from tudor times, there are some lovely panelled rooms and a great deal of antique furniture, many of the bedrooms have four posters and private bathrooms.

The whole setting is one of peace and tranquillity with award winning food and good wine.

The Court is perfectly located for the visitor to explore the charm and beauty of the Cotswold countryside

THE JENNY WREN
Restaurant & Tea Rooms

Quaint Tea Rooms & Restaurant.
Open 7 days a week, all day for full menu.
Morning coffee, hot & cold lunches.
Afternoon teas a speciality, Cornish cream teas.
Home cooking & baking.
Wide range of soft drinks, wines & beers.
Parties Welcome with Prior Booking.

Bed & Breakfast.
River Views, Tea/Coffee.
Twin or Double Rooms.

Picturesque walled garden with views of the famous Arlington Row.

11 The Street, Bibury. Tel: 01285 740555

Other Places of Interest...

The Village Hall used to be an old reading room which was built in 1878 on the site of the old church house which was used in 1636 as a poor house, and mentioned again for housing paupers in 1806.

The Primary School was built in 1845. The average attendance at that time was around 70. The building was enlarged to take more pupils in 1872, although during the twentieth century the numbers have declined due to an increase in retired people settling in Bibury.

The oldest house in the village is Pigeon House - so called in 1714 due to a medieval dovecote by its side, where pigeons used to roost. The house originates from the fourteenth or fifteenth century, and has a restored medieval chimney stack. It is located just off the hill up to Burford opposite the right turn to Coln St.Aldwyn.

The Jesus Almshouses in Bibury are found a little further down the hill on the same side of the road. They were founded by a Mr. Hugh Westwood, whose generosity on behalf of the poor in the Cotswolds was well known. Originally Mr. Westwood was a yeoman farmer from Chedworth who made his money dealing in land and property and who acquired a dubious reputation in business. In the sixteenth century he became the owner of the manors in Bibury and Arlington, having previously been a tenant of Oseney Abbey. The almshouses were intended for a master and three poor co-brethren. However, at the end of the 19th century the property was sold and the proceeds were invested. The interest from this investment going to support two needy men. Nowadays it is not often awarded! The old almshouse is now named 'Westwood Cottage'.

A Dipper

The Quarry Hill Ghosts.

Quarry Hill, up above the village of Bibury, is said to be a lurking place of restless spirits - the souls of those who have lived in the neighbourhood and cannot find peace in death. Among the apparitions seen, none has been seen more frequently and by more eyes than the white woman leading the white ox. For centuries she appears, and always unexpectedly. A manuscript from the thirteenth century may explain the mystery:

In the thirteenth century Barnsley was a chapelry of Bibury, and on festive days attendance was made at the mother church by the devout. The manuscript records that three widows refused to pay legacies due on the death of their husbands to the church at Bibury, and as a result were excommunicated. Two of the widows relented and paid the Church, but the third widow, Juliana, passed from earth unabsolved of her debt to the Church. To this day Juliana's unhappy and restless spirit appears leading a phantom ox (the ox being symbolic of the outstanding debt) wending her way towards Bibury Church as if to pay the legacy and so rest in peace. For centuries she has so appeared, generally on the eve of the Feast of St. Matthew.

Another strange tale is that of the Grey Lady of Arlington Mill. There was an old rich miller at Arlington Mill, whose wife had predeceased him leaving him with four grown up sons and an empty bed. A young Bibury girl called Mary was offered to him as a wife, and in the eyes of the village Mary had made a good match to the miller, who was wealthy and influential.

The eldest of the millers sons was called John, and he was a cobbler. He fell in love with Mary, and his love was returned. The Miller found out about their love affair and was so enraged that he fought with his son and threw him from the top of the mill building into the stream below, where he perished. It was a freezing January day and there was snow on the ground. He shut his wife out in the snow, forbidding anyone in the village to give her shelter. She hammered on the door of the Mill all night, weeping over the body of her lover. She was found frozen to death on the banks of the Coln. Her grey ghost can still be seen coming into the Mill and searching in vain for her lover.

Another ghost sighted on Quarry Hill is the Christmas Coach. In the latter part of the 18th Century, war fever induced many young men to join the forces. Two best friends from the Midlands, Teddy Harridge and Ned Taylor, decided to join the Navy. They took part in the capture of St. Lucia where Harridge escaped without injury, but poor Taylor was mortally wounded. Some time later in October 1796, Harridge started the journey home for Christmas, having said goodbye the grave of his friend in St. Lucia.

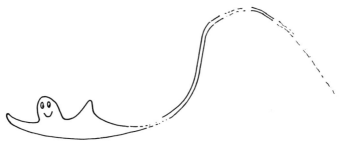

Many times on board ship the spirit of poor Ned was glimpsed. At 3.30 p.m. on Christmas Eve, Harridge boarded the coach at Cirencester to take him through Bibury and on to his family. As the coach approached Quarry Hill, the driver felt some disquiet. He saw ahead of him a pale procession crossing the road, and leading it was a pale woman leading a white ox (Juliana), followed by the grey lady of Arlington Mill and other lost souls. Last of all Harridge saw Ned Taylor, wearing his uniform. Harridge recognised his old friend as the horses reared up and bolted at the ghostly forms. The horses dashed down the hill into the millstream and the carriage was overturned. The coach driver was crushed to death, but fortunately Harridge survived and managed to make his way home to the Midlands. Each Christmas Eve the coach can be heard racing down Quarry Hill, but it never reaches the other side of the millstream. You may even glimpse the strange procession ....